ATTACK OF THE...

FOUL FUNGI

By William Anthony

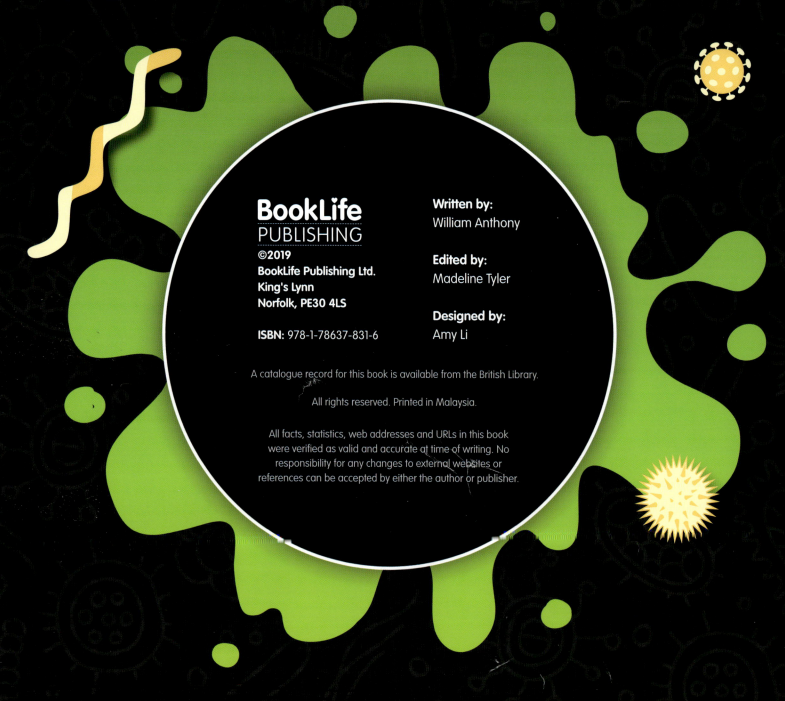

BookLife
PUBLISHING

©2019
BookLife Publishing Ltd.
King's Lynn
Norfolk, PE30 4LS

ISBN: 978-1-78637-831-6

Written by:
William Anthony

Edited by:
Madeline Tyler

Designed by:
Amy Li

A catalogue record for this book is available from the British Library.

All facts, statistics, web addresses and URLs in this book were verified as valid and accurate at time of writing. No responsibility for any changes to external websites or references can be accepted by either the author or publisher.

PHOTO CREDITS

529 889 88 8

CONTENTS

Words that look like <u>this</u> can be found in the glossary on page 24.

TRICKY WORDS

FUNGUS = singular (one fungus)

FUNGI = plural (many fungi)

FUNGAL = to do with a fungus or many fungi

BAD THINGS COME IN SMALL PACKAGES

Imagine the smallest thing you can. Now try to imagine something that's so small that you can't even see it. This is how small microorganisms are.

> Micro means tiny. Organism means a living thing.

ARGH!

Get the <u>microscope</u>! We need to look at these things more closely.

Microorganisms are sometimes called microbes, and they are everywhere. They're on the ground, in the air and in our water. They're even on our skin and inside our bodies.

FOUL FUNGI

TOADSTOOL

Fungi are a type of microbe. They are alive and some are too small to see. Some fungi are much bigger, such as toadstools.

"Fungi can grow that big? We're doomed!"

Fungi cannot make their own food. Instead, they break down dead plants and animals or feed off living ones.

"That poor tree. The fungi are taking over!"

Some fungi can be good. Yeast is a fungus that we use to make our bread rise. Other fungi live safely in our bodies.

The bread is okay, people.
The bread is okay!

Other fungi are not so good for us. Some can make us itch, give us rashes and even be <u>poisonous</u> to eat.

FUNGAL INFECTION

"The fungi <u>invasion</u> has begun. We need to find out more."

ATHLETE'S FOOT

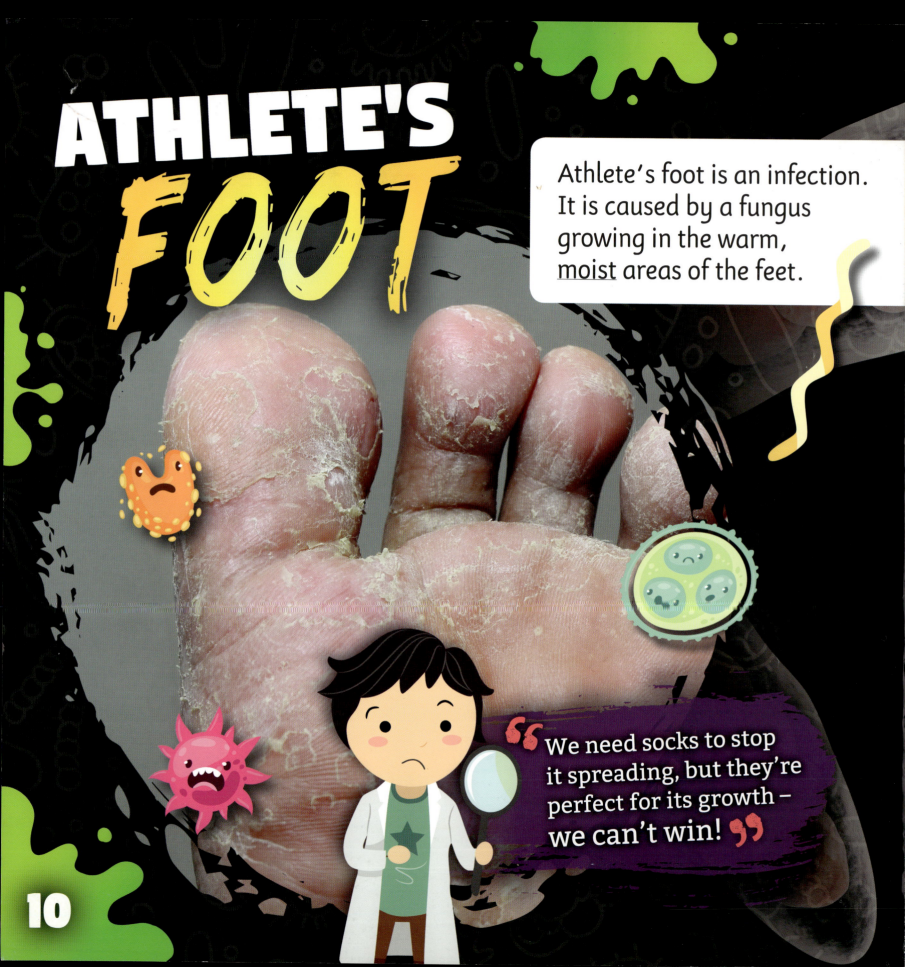

Athlete's foot is an infection. It is caused by a fungus growing in the warm, moist areas of the feet.

We need socks to stop it spreading, but they're perfect for its growth – we can't win!

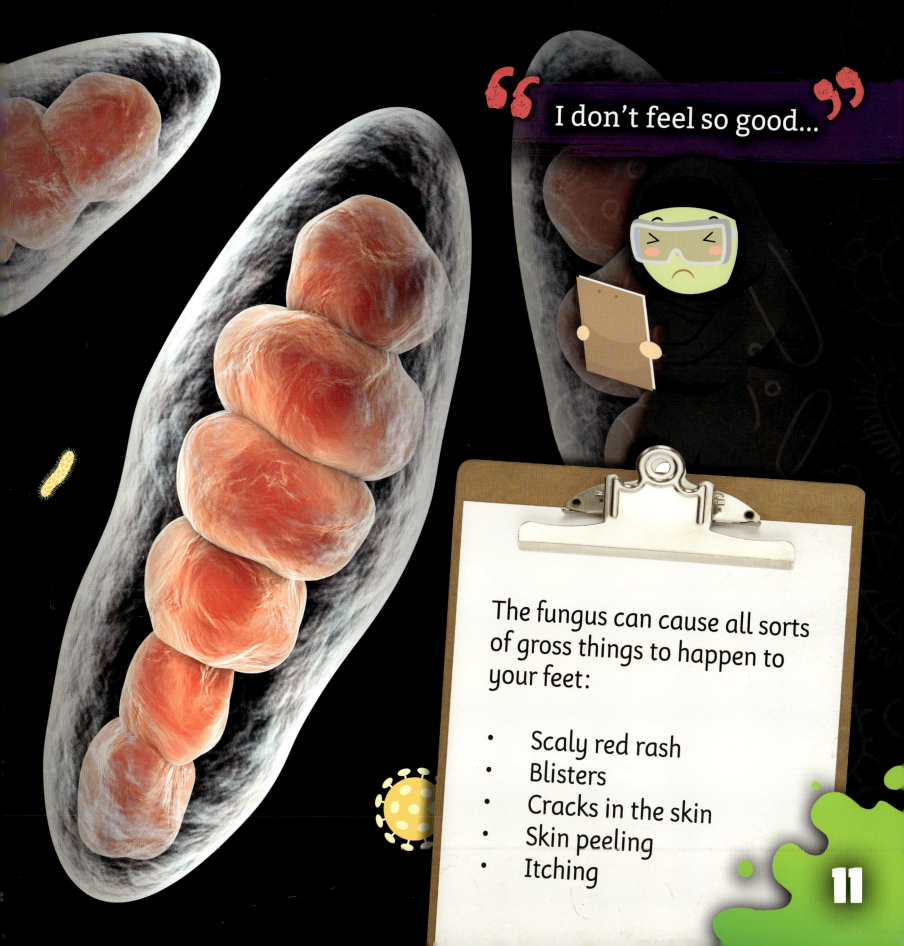

"I don't feel so good..."

The fungus can cause all sorts of gross things to happen to your feet:

- Scaly red rash
- Blisters
- Cracks in the skin
- Skin peeling
- Itching

11

RINGWORM

Ringworm is caused by the same fungus that causes athlete's foot. The fungus can live anywhere on the body, such as the hair, skin and nails.

"Ringworm can <u>spread</u> from person to person. I'm making a 'no hugging' rule."

Ringworm can cause lots of different things to happen to our bodies:

- Ring-shaped red marks
- Itching
- Scaly skin
- Spreading rash

It's called **ringworm** – it was never going to be good, was it?

ZOMBIE-ANT FUNGUS

Other animals are <u>affected</u> by fungi too. There is a type of fungus that can turn ants into <u>zombies</u>.

Zombie ants? Will somebody please get these fungi under control?

The fungus takes over the ant's whole body and controls it. It makes the ant walk to a leaf or a branch, where the fungus can feed and grow.

"The fungus is coming out of the top of the ant's head!"

JOCK ITCH

Fungi can reach everywhere on the human body. EVERYWHERE. Jock itch is a fungal infection that can grow in your groin or between your bum cheeks.

> Fungi grow best in warm places on the body, which is why even your bum isn't safe.

> **"** Of all the fungal infections so far, this is the one I want least. **"**

Jock itch can be found on your bottom and your thighs. It can cause:

- Redness
- Itching
- Burning feelings
- Rash
- Dry, peeling skin

17

HONEY FUNGUS

Fungi don't just invade animals. Plants can come under attack too. Some trees have to battle with honey fungus.

"How can something sound so nice but be so **horrid?**"

Honey fungus attacks the roots of a tree in order to kill it. It then feeds off the dead tree.

Fungi are killing plants now? Won't somebody please save us?

MOUTH *THRUSH*

A fungus called Candida is normally <u>harmless</u> to humans. However, it can cause an infection in your mouth called thrush.

"**Harmless?** Are you sure?"

CANDIDA

" There has to be a way we can <u>treat</u> this... "

Mouth thrush can be spotted quite easily. The fungus can cause:

- White spots
- Cracks in the corners of the mouth
- Things to taste differently
- Pain and difficulty eating

FIGHTING BACK

There are lots of ways that we can fight back against fungi. We can take tablets, use creams and even have <u>injections</u>.

" Wait, so we're not all doomed? "

Ha! Get back, fungi! I've got cream, and I'm not afraid to use it!

Tablets, creams and injections can kill off the fungus or stop it from growing and getting bigger. The fight back against fungi has begun!

GLOSSARY

affected   to have caused a change in something

harmless   not dangerous

infection   an illness caused by dirt or microbes getting into the body

injections   measured amounts of liquid medicine that are put into the body with a needle

invasion   when something comes into a place where it is not wanted or invited

microscope   a piece of scientific equipment that makes things look many times bigger

moist   slightly wet

poisonous   dangerous or deadly when eaten

spread   to move around from place to place to affect a larger area

treat   attempt to cure

zombies   a living thing that is controlled by something else

INDEX